FACT FILE

HEIGHT: 6 ft. 4 in.
FAVE T.V. PROGRAMME: Survival.
HOBBIES: Travel and wild boar wrestling.
FAVE FOOD: Crocodile steaks.
AMBITION: To become more famous than Tarzan!

MORGYN THE MIGHTY

FACT FILE

HEIGHT: 5 ft. 10 in.
HOBBIES: Table football and sport quizzes.
FAVE FOOD: The half-time pie!
AMBITION: To keep scoring goals
FAVOURITE TEAM: The one I'm playing for.

JIMMY GRANT

STARS IN VICTOR

£3.70

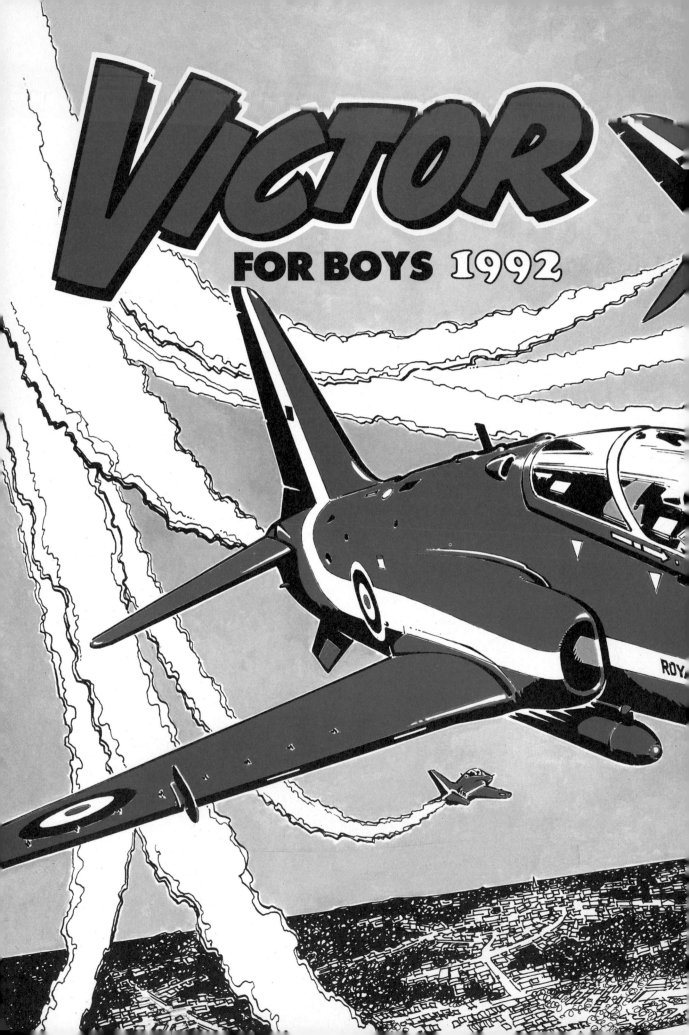

ALL THIS INSIDE—

Printed and Published in Great Britain by
D.C. Thomson & Co. Ltd., 185 Fleet Street,
London EC4A 2HS.
© D.C. Thomson & Co. Ltd. 1991.

ISBN 0-85116-512-5

OF THE TRACK

Alf Tupper, the runner known as the Tough of the Track, was competing in the 10,000 metres Longhurst Trophy race at Crystal Palace. For the first four laps the lead changed frequently, with no-one keen to make the running . . .

WHO IS THAT? DOESN'T HE KNOW THIS IS A 10,000 METRES RACE?

HE'S SAM SNELL, A BIT OF A DARK HORSE. HE SURE DOESN'T LIKE RUNNING WITH THE PACK.

MUST BE SOMETHING WE SAID!

9

Alf was eager to learn more about Sam Snell...

I'M A FELL RUNNER FROM UP SKIPDALEWAY, ALF. YOU WOULDN'T HAVE CAUGHT ME ON THE FELLS, THAT'S FOR SURE!

I'VE DONE A BIT OF FELL RUNNING MYSELF.

IT'S THE ALL-COMERS CHALLENGE ON SKIPDALE FELL IN A COUPLE OF WEEKS. WHY NOT ENTER AND I'LL PROVE MY POINT!

I MIGHT JUST DO THAT!

Alf, who ran his own one-man welding business, could never resist a challenge!

I RECKON I'M DUE A HOLIDAY, AND THEY SAY THE SCENERY'S GREAT UP SKIPDALE WAY.

Next day Alf headed north...

YOU'RE NOT GOING TO MAKE IT, ARE YOU, OLD GIRL? WE'LL TAKE A BREATHER.

ALF TUPPER WELDER AND METAL WORKER

GOOD DAY TO YOU! LOOKS LIKE YOU'VE GOT TROUBLE.

MY VAN'S NOT AS YOUNG AS SHE USED TO BE. I'M JUST LETTING HER COOL DOWN.

HEY, DAD! DO YOU KNOW WHO THAT IS?

YOU'RE ALF TUPPER — THE TOUGH OF THE TRACK!

THAT'S ME — I CANNOT TELL A LIE!

I SAW YOU RUN IN THE WATERFORD MILE LAST YEAR, ALF, AND IN THE FENBRIDGE TROPHY. I ALWAYS WANTED TO MEET YOU! I'M A RUNNER, TOO!

IS THAT A FACT?

I'LL RUN 'EM!

I RECKON YOU WILL AT THAT!

On the first Saturday, Alf went along with Tommy and Fred to the sheepdog trials . . .

ARE YOU GOING TO SHOW 'EM HOW IT'S DONE, THEN, JED?

YOU'LL WIN, JED! YOU'VE TRAINED WITH ALF TUPPER!

HE'S STILL YOUNG AND A WEE BIT WAYWARD, ALF.

Jed started well . . .

EASY NOW, JED! THAT'S THE WAY!

But as Jed made to pen the sheep he became excitable and they scattered . . .

HEEL, BOY! HEEL! COME BY!

HE'S A LOT TO LEARN. STILL, WE GOT FIFTH PLACE.

YOU TRIED, DIDN'T YOU, BOY?

During the following week Alf and Tommy trained hard . . .

THE WEATHER CAN GET PRETTY BAD UP HERE, ALF. THE MIST COMES DOWN LIKE A BLANKET SOMETIMES.

LET'S HOPE IT KEEPS FINE FOR NEXT SATURDAY.

So did the opposition!

WHAT'S KEEPING YOU, LADS?

SAM SNELL! WE'RE SAVING OURSELVES FOR SATURDAY, MATE!

12

THEY DON'T INTEND YOU TAKING A SHORT CUT. THEY MARK YOU WITH PAINT AT THE TOP!

AWAY YOU GO, LAD!

SAM LOOKS A LOT FRESHER THAN I FEEL — BLOOMIN' ADA! IT'S JED!

WHAT IS IT, BOY? YOU WANT ME TO FOLLOW YOU?

Jed led Alf to a bush-screened gully . . .

THERE'S A LAD DOWN THERE! IT'S TOMMY!

HE'S UNCONSCIOUS! HE MUST HAVE GONE OFF THE PATH IN THE MIST AND TAKEN A TUMBLE. BETTER NOT MOVE HIM.

Alf set off for help, the race forgotten . . .

STAY, BOY! STAY!

14

15

At the hospital . . .

TOMMY'S RIGHT LEG IS BROKEN, BUT APART FROM BRUISES HE HAS NO OTHER INJURIES.

WELL, THAT'S A RELIEF!

CAN WE TAKE HIM HOME?

Later, at the farmhouse . . .

THE MIST GOT REAL THICK ON THE TOP AND I STRAYED OFF THE PATH. ANYWAY, HOW DID YOU GET ON IN THE RACE, ALF?

RACE? BLOOMIN' ADA! I'D FORGOTTEN ALL ABOUT IT!

THERE'S SOMEONE AT THE DOOR.

WE WERE TOLD YOU WERE STAYING HERE, MR TUPPER. YOU FORGOT TO COLLECT THIS!

BLOOMIN' ADA!

YOU WON, ALF!

HE WENT PAST ME LIKE THE DEVIL HIMSELF WAS AFTER HIM. AND I THOUGHT HE WAS TIRED!

YES, WELL I RECKON TOMMY HAD SOMETHING TO DO WITH THAT!

WE'LL GET OUR PHOTOS IN THE PAPER! COR, THIS WAS WORTH BREAKING A LEG FOR!

WELL, DON'T MAKE A HABIT OF IT, TOMMY. JED MIGHT NOT BE AROUND TO HELP OUT NEXT TIME!

16

The End

PETER ELLIOTT

1. Elliott was born in 1952, 1962 or 1972?

2. Can you fill in the remaining letters to discover his home town? R---E---M.

3. Did he win a bronze, silver or gold medal in the Seoul Olympics 1500 metres?

4. When he's not running, is Peter Elliott a skilled joiner, computer engineer or welder (like Alf Tupper!)?

5. He struck gold in the 1990 Commonwealth Games, but which medal did he win in the 1986 Commonwealth Games 800 metres?

ANSWERS

1. 1962. 2. Rotherham. 3. Silver. 4. Joiner. 5. Bronze.

17

That evening at the London office of Sir James Morris, Controller of Force Five —

PARIS? WHAT'S IT GOT TO DO WITH US?

IT SEEMS THE TERRORISTS WERE BRITISH, SIR JAMES. THEY WERE TRYING TO FINANCE THEIR ORGANISATION HERE. WE'VE ALREADY HAD THREATS FROM THE ONES WHO GOT AWAY!

THEY WANT THEIR OWN MAN BACK — OR ELSE. IT'S A JOB FOR YOU — AND FORCE FIVE.

Each member of Force Five had a special micro-chip embedded in one of his teeth. It vibrated when they were needed. Character actor Barry Martin was one of the team . . .

THIS IS WHERE YOU GET YOURS, PAL!

A BUZZ! OF ALL THE TIMES FOR SIR JAMES TO CALL!

ARRRGH!

BANG!

THIS IS THE LAST ACT. I CAN BE AT HQ IN HALF-AN-HOUR . . .

Butch McGraw was a star player in American football's British League . . .

CRUMP

A BUZZ FROM SIR JAMES! NICE TIMING. THE GAME SHOULD BE OVER IN THREE MINUTES!

'Brains' Tyler, technical genius, and ace pilot and air-cargo boss 'Greasy' Wilson were both part of Force Five.

IS THERE ANYTHING YOU CAN'T DO WITH ELECTRONICS, BRAINS? THE PLANE'S CONTROLS RESPOND ALMOST AS I THINK ABOUT IT!

NO PROBLEM. NOW LET'S GET TO SIR JAMES.

STAND BACK! THIS MAN IS BADLY BURNED!

ARE YOU HURT?

OF COURSE HE'S NOT! HE'S DONE THAT STUNT TOO MANY TIMES IN SOME OF MY OLD FILMS.

TV AND NEWSPAPERS WILL ALL CARRY THE STORY OF HOW WHEELS ROGERS WAS FLOWN BACK TO LONDON FOR EMERGENCY TREATMENT . . .

Later, Barry — an expert at theatrical make-up — disguised himself as the terrorist.

EXCEPT THAT IT WON'T BE WHEELS WRAPPED-UP IN ALL THOSE BANDAGES. IT'LL BE OUR NASTY LITTLE TERRORIST! THE REST IS UP TO YOU LOT . . .

THAT OUGHT TO DO IT.

YOU'D FOOL HIS OWN MOTHER!

MY PALS WILL HAVE ME FREE IN NO TIME.

WE'RE USING ONE OF WILSON'S PLANES, TAKING-OFF FROM A SMALL CIVIL 'DROME EAST OF PARIS. THERE'S A SORT OF AIR-DISPLAY GOING ON THERE AT THE MOMENT. WE'RE LETTING IT BE LEAKED CAREFULLY. WITH LUCK HIS PALS WILL HAVE A GO AT RESCUING HIM.

Next morning —

NOT A SIGN!

IF THEY'RE SMART IT WON'T HAPPEN WHEN WE EXPECT IT. LET'S GO!

22

25

27

THE REAL THING

Lucky Chance returned safely and while the crew were heading off for some well-earned grub—

HEY, WHAT'S GOIN' ON OVER THERE?

FORGOTTEN, CHUCK? WAYNE STEWART, THE FILM STAR'S JOININ' THE SQUADRON TODAY.

Chuck Hanson was Lucky Chance's navigator.

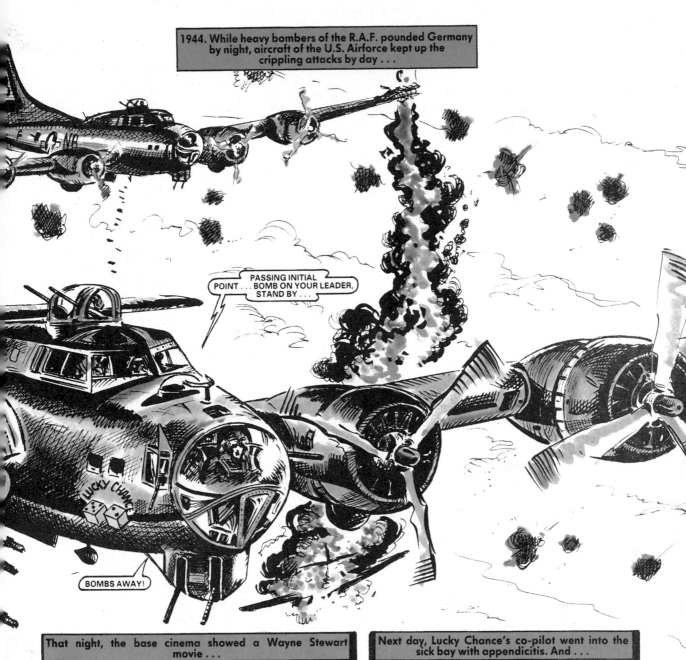

1944. While heavy bombers of the R.A.F. pounded Germany by night, aircraft of the U.S. Airforce kept up the crippling attacks by day . . .

PASSING INITIAL POINT . . . BOMB ON YOUR LEADER, STAND BY . . .

BOMBS AWAY!

That night, the base cinema showed a Wayne Stewart movie . . .

HUH! THAT WAYNE STEWART'S WINNIN' THE WAR SINGLE-HANDED!

RECKON WE CAN ALL GO HOME NOW!

WHAT A LOADA GARBAGE!

Next day, Lucky Chance's co-pilot went into the sick bay with appendicitis. And . . .

HI, I'M WAYNE STEWART. SEEMS LIKE I'M YOUR NEW CO-PILOT.

OH, YEH? WELL, JUST REMEMBER THIS AINT NO FILM SET, BUSTER . . .

... THE BULLETS UP THERE ARE THE REAL THING, SO YOU'D BETTER MEASURE UP!

WELL! I SURE UPSET HIM.

DON'T WORRY . . . CHUCK JES' DON'T LIKE NEW CO-PILOTS. I'M FRANKIE ZANELLO, LUCKY'S SKIPPER.

With Wayne at the controls Lucky Chance went on a test flight next day.

HE'S GOT A TOUCH LIKE A FLIPPIN' GORILLA.

SHUT UP, CHUCK!

A day or two later they took off for a raid on Germany . . .

FIGHTERS! TWELVE O'CLOCK HIGH!

MORE OF 'EM — TEN O'CLOCK CLOSING!

CLOSE IT UP, YOU GUYS! MOVE IT!

FLAMIN' FLAK JACKETS . . . LOOK AT THOSE KRAUTS GO!

ZOOOMPH!

SHEZOOOMPH!

FIGHTERS ON THE LEFT! ROCKETS COMIN' IN!

GEE . . . RETURN TICKET'S GONE!

NO WONDER THAT NAVIGATOR RESENTS ME! IT'S EASY TO BE A CELLULOID HERO . . . BUT IT'S DIFFERENT WHEN YOU FACE THE REAL THING.

30

As they turned for home . . .

WE GOT AN ESCORT!

THAT'LL KEEP THOSE KRAUTS AT BAY!

HOW'S THE SKIPPER? OXYGEN OKAY?

HE'S FINE, 'CEPT THERE'S NO FEELING IN HIS LEGS.

As they crossed the North Sea—

PORT INNER'S SEIZED UP. WE'RE LOSING HEIGHT. THROW EVERYTHING OUT — GUNS, RADIOS — ANYTHING.

Their nearest airfield was a fighter station with a short runway . . .

CO-PILOT TO CREW. I'LL NEED TO KEEP LOADSA POWER ON WHEN WE COME IN OR SHE'LL STALL, SO I'LL NEED ONE OF YOU TO HELP WITH THE BRAKES. THE REST OF YOU'D BETTER BALE OUT. WE'VE JUST ENOUGH HEIGHT.

NAVIGATOR HERE. I'LL STAY.

Soon the airfield came into view—

WHEN WE'RE ON THE GROUND, CHUCK, HIT THOSE BRAKES HARD WHEN I SAY!

YOU'RE THE BOSS!

Chuck hit the brakes on Wayne's signal but seconds later—

DARN IT! THE UNDERCARRIAGE HAS COLLAPSED!

Lucky Chance skidded off the runway where the perimeter fence brought them to a stop!

THAT WAS A GREAT PIECE OF FLYIN', WAYNE. I NEVER SAID BEFORE, BUT MY KID BROTHER IS ONE OF YOUR BIGGEST FANS . . . AND I GUESS THAT GOES FOR THE REST OF THE CREW NOW!

THANKS, CHUCK. IT WASN'T BAD FOR A GUY WITH A TOUCH LIKE A GORILLA!

THE END

FOOTBALL PHOTO FUN

SO LET'S SEE WHO'S GOT THE HARDEST HEAD THEN!

I SAID STAND STILL AND I MEANT STAND STILL!

I DON'T CARE WHAT IT LOOKED LIKE FROM UP THERE — FROM DOWN HERE IT WAS A FOUL!

IF YOU WANT THIS CUP YOU'LL HAVE TO FIGHT FOR IT!

I DON'T CARE IF THREE IS YOUR LUCKY NUMBER!

With time running out, Scotland went for the winner . . .

But . . .

THE GOALIE'S BEATEN!

McCAIL'S SCORED! GOT TO BE!

FANTASTIC DEFENDING!

OFF THE LINE!

36

38

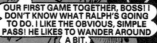

Before the match . . .

WE'VE A BIG SUPPORT OUT THERE — SO GO OUT AND PLAY FOOTBALL!

MAGIC. I PLAY BETTER WHEN THE FANS CHEER YOU ON! IS IT THE SAME WITH YOU, JIMMY?

SAME FOR ALL OF US, RALPH!

But England got off to a slow start . . .

WAKE UP, ENGLAND! DON'T GET CAUGHT IN POSSESSION!

Later . . .

CHASE IT, RALPH! AND HOLD IT UNTIL SOMEONE GETS UP WITH YOU.

But . . .

YOU CAN'T SCORE FROM THAT ANGLE, YOU DOUGH-NUT!

HE SHOULD HAVE PULLED IT BACK.

Then . . .

YOU'VE GIVEN IT AWAY, YOU MEAT-HEAD!

WHY DIDN'T HE PUSH IT OUT HERE TO ME? MUCH EASIER!

HE'D BE A GREAT PLAYER, IF ONLY HIS TEAM-MATES KNEW WHAT HE WAS GOING TO DO WITH THE BALL!

THAT'S GONE NOWHERE, CLAYTON! RUBBISH!

SEE THAT? RALPH DOES IT EVERY TIME! HIS RIGHT ELBOW STICKS OUT... AND HE KNOCKS THE BALL LEFT!

YEAH! SO WHAT?

Jimmy paused the film again...

THERE HE GOES AGAIN... STICKING THAT ELBOW OUT AND MOVING THE BALL LEFT.

YEAH. I SEE WHAT YOU MEAN!

WHEN HE DRIBBLES, HE DRAGS THE BALL AWAY WITH HIS RIGHT, FLIPS IT ACROSS TO HIS LEFT FOOT AND HITS IT RIGHT! EVERY TIME THE SAME!

England's last tour match was against Sweden...

IT'S GOING TO BE OKAY, RALPH! I'VE FIGURED OUT YOUR GAME!

OH, YEAH? WHAT DO I HAVE TO DO?

NOTHING! JUST PLAY IN YOUR USUAL STYLE. LEAVE THE REST TO ME!

BIG CROWD FROM HOME HERE AGAIN TODAY, LADS! GIVE 'EM A TREAT!

IF I DON'T PLAY WELL, TAKE ME OFF AND PUT THE SUB ON! I HATE BEING BOOED!

IT WON'T COME TO THAT, RALPH!

The England fans were in good form!

ENGLAND! ENGLAND!

44

45

The End

How d'you like the fifties-style strip and heavy leather boots? When the ball was kicked with boots like these, it went for miles!

Football is now part of the fashion business, with clubs changing their strip designs practically every year!

GETT IN G

Faster and fitter than ever before, today's sportsmen enjoy facilities and opportunities stars in the past could only dream about.

As our pictures show, the gear they wear and the equipment they use has changed with the times as well!

In its day, this Grand Prix car was a winner . . .

ack in 1964, ski
mp champ
eikko
ankkonen
ore a woollen
at and
oves . . .

. but in 1991 a
rotective
elmet and a hi-
ech, skintight
ki-suit is just
hat the skier
rdered!

Looking more like a waiter
than a top class sprinter,
Linford Christie strides to
victory!

. . . but it would
be no match for
the high-
performance cars
of the nineties!

BLOOMIN' ADA, I'LL
STICK TO MY USUAL
GEAR, MATE!

PETER BEARDSLEY

1. Beardsley first made his name with Newcastle United, but can you name his first senior club?

2. Before signing for Newcastle, he played abroad. Can you name the country?

3. How big was the transfer fee when Liverpool signed Beardsley?

4. Peter Beardsley's favourite TV "soap" is "Neighbours", "Eastenders", or "Coronation Street"?

5. He won his first England cap against which country?

ANSWERS

1. Carlisle United. 2. Canada (Vancouver Whitecaps). 3. £1.9 million (making him at that time the most expensive player in the Football League). 4. Eastenders. 5. Against Egypt, when he came on as substitute.

CADMAN
THE FRONT-LINE COWARD

World War One. British troops in Flanders were making a desperate fighting retreat from a massive German attack. Captain Gerald Cadman, V.C. was just retreating!

VORWAERTS! STORM THE TRENCH!

GAD! I'M GETTING OUT OF HERE!

NEVER SEEN A TOMMY OFFICER RUN AWAY SO FAST!

WHY WASTE AMMUNITION ON SUCH A COWARD?

Corporal Tom Smith had also spotted Cadman's rapid retreat!

THE CAPTAIN'S REALLY HOPPED IT THIS TIME! JUST WHEN THE GOING GETS TOUGH!

JERRIES HAVE BURST THROUGH ALL AROUND US! NOW THE BLINKING GUN'S JAMMED!

CEASE FIRE, TOMMY!

AAH!

Later . . .

THE GERMANS HAVE MOVED ON. THEY MUST HAVE CAPTURED CAPTAIN CADMAN!

THE LIEUTENANT HERE COULDN'T HAVE SEEN THE WAY THAT BLIGHTER WAS RUNNING!

Next day . . .

THE WHOLE FRONT HAS BROKEN. MUST GET AS FAR AWAY FROM THE FIGHTING AS POSSIBLE!

OPEN WARFARE NOW. NO TRENCHES. ALLIED AND ENEMY UNITS SCATTERED ALL OVER THE PLACE.

That evening . . .

URRH! GRENADE!

HUNS!

KAMERAD! I SURRENDER!

KAMERAD? YOU'RE NO COMRADE OF OURS, CHUM!

WHAT THE DEUCE ARE OUR CHAPS DOING WITH THESE HUNS?

THESE ARE OUR PALS NOW, SEE.

LOT MORE OF US BACK IN THOSE WOODS.

FRENCH, BRITISH AND GERMANS ALL CAMPED HERE! DESERTERS FROM BOTH SIDES BANDING TOGETHER TO LIVE LIKE OUTLAWS!

I'M JUST KNOWN AS SARGE. ME AND BIG JODI HERE RUN THIS MOB BETWEEN US.

UND WE SHOOT ALL OFFIZIERS!

HOLD ON, I'M A DESERTER MYSELF. WHY ELSE WOULD A CAPTAIN BE RIDING A DESPATCH BIKE?

YOU'LL NEED TO PROVE THAT TO STAY ALIVE . . . SIR!

Later . . .

WE'RE GONNA RAID A BRITISH SUPPLY DUMP BEFORE THE ADVANCING JERRIES CAPTURE IT. YOU'RE GOING TO HELP US.

NOW HOW THE DEUCE DO I GET OUT OF THIS?

At the dump . . .

VORWAERTS! CHARGE!

UURGH!

FALL BACK! FIRE OUR DEMOLITION CHARGES!

AAAGH!

GAD! THE DUMP'S BLOWING UP!

EXPLOSIF WIRES ALL CUT!

GET ON AND DRIVE US OUT SIR!

MUST SHOW MYSELF WILLING OR THESE SWINE WILL KILL ME!

GIVE 'EM A FEW PARTING SHOTS!

HOLD YOUR FIRE!

BUT WE COULD HAVE POTTED A FEW OF 'EM, CORP!

OFFICER'S ORDERS, LADS.

Later . . .

I RECKON ONE OF THE OFFICERS FROM MY OWN UNIT HAS BEEN CAPTURED BY THAT DESERTER MOB. PERMISSION TO GO OFF AND ASSIST HIM, SIR?

WHY NOT? WE'VE NOTHING LEFT TO GUARD HERE! GOOD LUCK!

THAT WAS CAPTAIN CADMAN DRIVING — OR MY NAME'S NOT TOM SMITH!

THAT MOB CAME ON FOOT, SO THEIR CAMP CAN'T BE FAR AWAY.

Meanwhile . . .

WE'VE DONE WELL. BAGS OF AMMO AND RATIONS, JODI!

JA, AND TRANSPORT FOR OUR NEXT RAID.

Two of the deserters began to argue . . .

NEIN! THIS IS MINE!

I'LL SLIP AWAY WHILE THOSE ROGUES QUARREL.

DIE, SCHWEIN!

GAD!

AAARGH!

MINE, HERR OFFIZIER! I MUST HAVE DROPPED IN THE LORRY. IT IS — HOW YOU SAY? . . . WORTH A PACKET. YOU WANT TAKE FROM ME?

NO — ER — CERTAINLY NOT!

TOO RISKY TRYING TO ESCAPE FROM THESE MURDEROUS RUFFIANS YET.

At dawn . . .

I HOPPED IT FROM THAT DUMP YOU RAIDED. ANY CHANCE OF JOINING UP WITH YOUR LOT?

TAKE HIM TO SARGE AND JODI.

GAD! SMITH! A DESERTER? NEVER! HE'S ALWAYS LOYAL TO ME, IF ONLY BECAUSE I OWN THE COTTAGE WHERE HIS FAMILY LIVES ON MY ESTATES BACK HOME.

I WON'T ASK WHAT YOU'RE DOING WITH THIS MOB, SIR, BUT I'LL DO ME BEST TO GET YOU BACK TO OUR OWN UNIT.

BACK TO FACE COURT-MARTIAL CHARGES? OH, NO, YOU WON'T, SMITH!

YOU'LL BE SHOT ON THE SPOT WHEN I TELL THESE RUFFIANS THAT YOU'RE ONLY A FAKE DESERTER!

But then . . .

URRH! SHELL FIRE!

JERRIES ATTACKING! BREAK CAMP!

CLEAR OUT THAT RABBLE AND OCCUPY THE WOODS!

NICE TO BE TOGETHER AGAIN, AIN'T IT, SIR?

NOT FOR LONG, SMITH!

55

Soon, at a nearby village . . .

ALL QUIET HERE, JODI.

JA, UNTIL WE LOOT THE PLACE!

RAUS! ALL OUT!

SHOOT 'EM DOWN!

YOU ARE BRITISH OFFICER! SAVE US!

HE WOULDN'T SAVE HIS OWN GRANNY! BUT THESE POOR FOLKS COULD GET MURDERED . . .

WHY HAVE THEY LEFT THESE BLOKES HERE?

TO GUARD THE LORRY OR WHATEVER'S UNDER THAT COVER?

OUT! ORDER OF THE BOOT!

UGH!

The End

CAN YOU SOLVE THIS CRIME BEFORE THE

CRIMEBUSTER

Private Detective Rick Chance — action man and modern day Sherlock Holmes. Case No. 985 for the Chance Enquiry agency gave him the chance to prove it!

It all began when a man fell overboard from a cross-Channel ferry . . .

NO TRACE OF LOST CHANNEL TRAVELLER

AAH!

Rick Chance had a visitor . . .

MY NAME IS NIGEL WILSON. HAROLD ROGERS, THE MAN WHO FELL OVERBOARD FROM THE FERRY, WAS A CLIENT OF MY LEGAL COMPANY. HE LEFT A LETTER TO BE OPENED IN THE EVENT OF HIS DEATH.

SINCE HE IS PRESUMED DEAD I'D LIKE TO HEAR WHAT THE LETTER HAS TO SAY, MISTER WILSON.

IN THIS LETTER HE ADMITS TO HAVING TAKEN PART WITH A MAN NAMED BILLY COWAN IN THE ROBBERY OF A SECURITY VEHICLE NEAR CHELMSFORD IN JUNE LAST YEAR.

WALTER, DIG INTO YOUR WONDERFUL MACHINE FOR ANY DETAILS WE HAVE.

YOU WILL SEE THAT HE BLAMES COWAN FOR THE SHOOTING OF ONE OF THE GUARDS.

HE SAYS . . . IT WAS DONE BEFORE I COULD STOP HIM. WE GOT TWO SACKS OF BANKNOTES FROM THE SECURITY VAN, BUT I WAS MAD WITH BILLY ABOUT THE SHOOTING . . .

"I let him know when we switched cars after the robbery . . ."

YOU'RE CRAZY! YOU SHOULDN'T HAVE USED THE GUN.

GOING SOFT ON ME, EH? GETTING READY TO SQUEAL THAT IT WAS ME USED THE SHOOTER TO THE COPS, MAYBE.

ARGH!

I AIN'T RISKING THAT, MATE.

"He left me for dead, but the bullet had turned off one of my ribs. I avoided the police and got back to town, where I heard about Billy being killed..."

THE CAR OVERTURNED WHEN TRYING TO CRASH THROUGH A POLICE ROADBLOCK.

WE HAVE IT. THE MONEY STOLEN WAS TWO MILLION IN USED NOTES. IT WASN'T FOUND IN THE WRECKED CAR AND POLICE OPINION IS THAT IT'S IN THE POSSESSION OF THE UNKNOWN ACCOMPLICE.

WHICH IS DENIED BY THIS LETTER FROM THIS MAN WHO CLAIMS TO HAVE BEEN THAT ACCOMPLICE.

HE CONTINUES... I WANT TO PUT THE RECORD STRAIGHT. I RECKON COWAN HID THE MONEY SOMEWHERE BETWEEN WHERE HE LEFT ME AND WHERE HE WAS KILLED. MAYBE THIS LETTER WILL BE SOME HELP IN FINDING IT. I'D LIKE THE INSURANCE REWARD TO GO TO THE FAMILY OF THE DEAD GUARD.

SO THAT'S THE STORY, MR CHANCE. WILL YOU TAKE ON THE CASE?

I DON'T SEE HOW I CAN TURN DOWN A RETAINER FROM DAVY JONES' LOCKER. WALTER, I'VE LISTED A FEW JOBS FOR YOU WHILE I'M BUSY.

I'LL COME WITH YOU, IF YOU DON'T MIND. TWO MILLION IS A LOT OF MONEY.

THERE ARE SO MANY PLACES WHERE COWAN COULD HAVE STOPPED TO HIDE THE MONEY.

NOT SO MANY IF YOU CONSIDER THAT A ROBBER WON'T PART FROM HIS LOOT WITHOUT GOOD REASON. FIND THAT REASON AND WE FIND THE MONEY.

An hour of Rick's fast driving later...

THAT'S WHERE THEY CHANGED CARS AND COWAN SHOT HIS PARTNER. NOW WE GO ON TO WHERE COWAN CRASHED THE CHANGE CAR, BECAUSE OF HIS BAD DRIVING ON A TIGHT BEND.

Fifteen minutes later...

SEE THAT TREE? THIS MUST BE THE SPOT. NOW WE PICTURE BILLY COWAN WITH A WRECKED CAR AND TWO HEAVY SACKS OF MONEY.

61

THIS IS DOWNLEA FARM, WHERE COWAN STOLE ANOTHER CAR. IT'S ON A BEND OF THE SAME LANE LEADING TO THE MOTORWAY.

WE'LL GO THERE AS COWAN DID — ON FOOT ACROSS THE MEADOW.

Rick had a word with the farmer . . .

THE PAPERS SAY YOU DIDN'T ACTUALLY SEE THE ROBBER, SIR! SO YOU CAN'T TELL US IF HE WAS CARRYING ANYTHING . . .

ALL I CAN TELL YOU IS THAT I HEARD MY CAR STARTING UP AND RAN OUT TO SEE HIM DRIVING OFF. I TELEPHONED THE POLICE . . .

"... and then heard later about him being killed trying to crash through a police roadblock on the motorway."

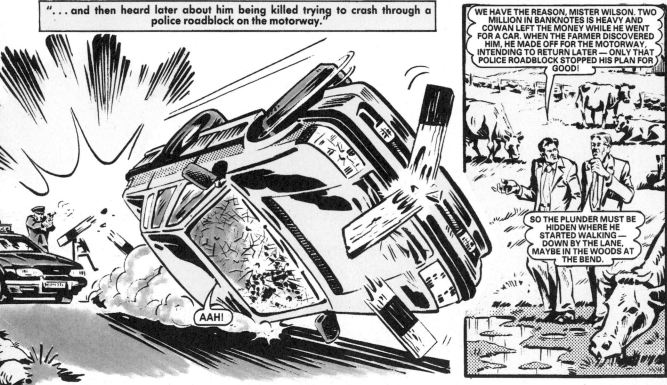

AAH!

WE HAVE THE REASON, MISTER WILSON. TWO MILLION IN BANKNOTES IS HEAVY AND COWAN LEFT THE MONEY WHILE HE WENT FOR A CAR. WHEN THE FARMER DISCOVERED HIM, HE MADE OFF FOR THE MOTORWAY, INTENDING TO RETURN LATER — ONLY THAT POLICE ROADBLOCK STOPPED HIS PLAN FOR GOOD!

SO THE PLUNDER MUST BE HIDDEN WHERE HE STARTED WALKING — DOWN BY THE LANE, MAYBE IN THE WOODS AT THE BEND.

NOT THE WOODS. TOO OBVIOUS. NO, COWAN WOULD LOOK FOR A MORE SECURE PLACE, WHERE ALL TRACE OF HIDING COULD BE REMOVED.

THE TROUGH! HE COULD HAVE DUG INTO THE MUD UNDER IT. THAT'S IT!

GLAD TO HAVE BEEN OF HELP, MISTER WILSON, THOUGH I DOUBT IF THAT IS YOUR NAME. AND IT'S NOT HAROLD ROGERS, THAT INNOCENT TRAVELLER WHOSE IDENTITY YOU BORROWED FOR THAT FORGED LETTER . . .

HUH! YOU KNEW!

HAVE YOU SOLVED THE MYSTERY? TURN TO PAGE 64 TO FIND OUT!

ACTION STATIONS!
A TRUE WAR STORY

In August 1942, during the Second World War, a convoy sets out from Gibraltar to take vitally needed supplies to the beleaguered island of Malta. In the convoy is the tanker Ohio, whose cargo is needed to keep the island's planes flying. On the 11th August, the German and Italian forces carry out their first attack on the convoy and from then until it reaches Malta the ships are under almost constant air and seaborne assault.

On the evening of the 12th, the Ohio is torpedoed and badly damaged, but in an hour her crew have her under way again and next morning she rejoins the convoy. Next day part of a stricken German bomber lands on her and again her engines break down. An attempt is made to tow Ohio but it fails and the crew are taken off. The crew board again but when the tanker is again hit they have to abandon ship once more.

But Ohio will not die! Again the crew board and, fighting off attack after attack, she struggles on with a destroyer and minesweeper lashed to either side. Eventually, two days after the remainder of the convoy, Ohio reaches Malta to a tumultuous reception. Within hours of her arrival, the island's aircraft are airborne, thanks to the vital supplies she carried.

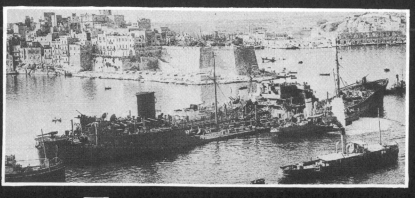

BIKER

Gary Jones, one of the youngest and best riders in big time motor-cycle racing, was pushing himself and his Sabre superbike hard in a challenge prize event on the fast Goldstone track . . .

ONLY TWO LAPS TO GO! TIME TO MAKE MY MOVE!

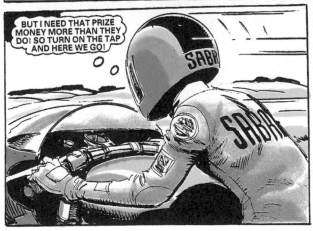

66

70

BAGS OF PUNCH IN THE OLD POWER POTS!

MAYBE TOO MUCH TOP-END POWER! CARRIED ME WIDE ON THIS CORNER!

STILL GETTING A VIBRO MASSAGE! I MUST BE NUTS TO RISK SUCH A HARD RACE ON THAT MAKESHIFT REPAIR JOB!

I'LL CUT IN PAST THESE WORKS RIDERS.

I'M BLOCKED BY THESE FALCO JOKERS! THERE'S STILL ROOM TO OVERTAKE BUT I'D BETTER WATCH OUT. THEIR TEAM OFTEN PULLS DODGY STUNTS!

The End

VICTOR
SPORTS QUIZ
ALAIN PROST

1. In which sport did Prost excel before he became a motor racing star?

2. He is nicknamed "The Predator", "The Professor" or "The Plunderer"?

3. Prost first won the Formula One World Championship in 1983, 1984 or 1985?

4. Can you name the year when he next won the World Championship?

5. Prost won the World Championship for the third time in which year?

ANSWERS

1. Football. He was on the books of a French club, but had to give up the game because of a knee injury. 2. The Professor. 3. 1985. 4. 1986. 5. 1989.

ENEMIES

...rking U-boat joined in the attack.

TORPEDO, SIR!

The Richmond was hit amidships.

AAAHH!

Hit in the leg, Don Sheppard was fighting for his life.

HELP ME!

Minutes? Hours? Time was a painful blur. Then helping hands were reaching out to him.

PLEASE HELP ME!

YOU ARE ALL RIGHT?

MY LEG, MATE. GOT HIT IN THE LEG.

IT IS DEEP WOUND. YOU LOSE MUCH BLOOD.

YOU'RE A JERRY! A LOUSY JERRY!

YOU MURDERING RAT! GET YOUR FILTHY HANDS OFF ME!

YOU — YOU ARE CHOKING ME!

YOU'RE DARN RIGHT, I'M CHOKING YOU . . . AAAAARGH!

When Don came round . . .

MY LEG! IT HURTS!

YOU WERE LOSING BLOOD. YOU WOULD HAVE DIED. I APPLIED A TOURNIQUET!

WHY? YOU'RE A JERRY! YOU MACHINE-GUN HELPLESS MEN IN THE WATER!

I HAVE NEVER MACHINE-GUNNED ANYONE. I AM ENGINEER ON U62 BEFORE DEPTH CHARGES FORCE US TO ABANDON SHIP.

YOU TIED MY HANDS! I SUPPOSE YOU WERE PLANNING TO PUT ME OVER THE SIDE!

I TIE YOUR HANDS TO STOP YOU ATTACKING ME. I SUGGEST WE CALL TRUCE UNTIL WE ARE PICKED UP. IF BRITISH SHIP — I WILL BE YOUR PRISONER. IF GERMAN — YOU WILL BE MINE.

THE FOOD HAS BEEN LOST. WE HAVE ONLY FOUR BOTTLES OF WATER. WE WILL SHARE THEM. I AM HERMAN LIEZT.

SHEPPARD — DON SHEPPARD.

A day passed by — two, three . . .

THIS IS FREDA. WE WERE TO BE MARRIED ON MY LAST LEAVE. SHE TOLD ME SHE HAD SOMEONE ELSE.

THAT'S THE TROUBLE WITH WOMEN, MATE. CAN'T TRUST 'EM. OH! MY LEG! CAN'T FEEL IT NOW.

WE MUST KEEP RELEASING THE TOURNIQUET. WE'RE GOING TO MAKE IT, DON. SOON WE WILL BE PICKED UP.

WATER GONE! MUST HAVE WATER!

GOING TO DIE . . . NO ONE WILL COME . . .

THEY WILL COME! YOU HAVE MY WATER. DRINK, DON!

Another day —

HELP US! PLEASE HELP US!

And then at last — rescue.

A SHIP, DON! A SHIP!

The U.S.S. Endurance.

TWO OF THEM, SIR. ONE BRITISH AND — HEY, THE OTHER'S A KRAUT!

HAUL 'EM UP!

EASY THERE, FELLER. YOU'RE GOING TO BE ALL RIGHT.

LOOK AFTER HIM. HE GAVE ME HIS WATER!

THIS MAN IS DEAD. HE'S GOT A HOLE IN HIM YOU COULD PUT YOUR FIST THROUGH.

BUT HE CAN'T BE. HE — HE SAVED MY LIFE. I HAD NO IDEA HE WAS HURT . . .

NOT TO WORRY. THE ONLY GOOD GERMAN IS A DEAD GERMAN, EH, FELLER? URRGH!

WHAT THE BLUE BLAZES GOT INTO HIM, DO YOU RECKON?

TOO MUCH SUN, I GUESS.

80

The End

JIMMY GRANT'S FOOTBALL PUZZLERS

FAMOUS TEAMS ★★★★★★★★★★

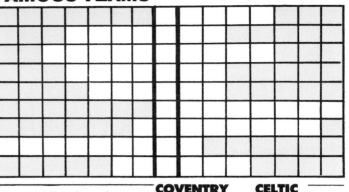

Can you fill in these famous football clubs on the grid so that the letters between the thick lines form another famous club?

COVENTRY
RANGERS
ASTON VILLA
LEEDS

CELTIC
PLYMOUTH
WIMBLEDON
WOLVES

HEARTS

★★★★★★★★★★★★★★★★★★★★★★★★★

hat the manager might say his team after a victory—

D 1

Every player likes to take part in a tournament. Can you spell 30 or more four-letter words by using only the letters in **TOURNAMENT?**

WHICH PLAYER SCORED?

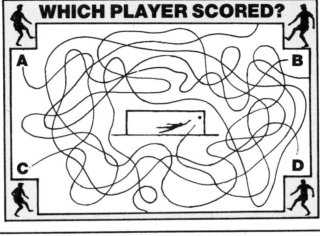

WORD LADDER

Can you change 'shot' to 'goal' in five steps, changing one letter at a time?

SHOT

_____
_____
_____
_____

GOAL

CAN YOU SPOT FIVE DIFFERENCES BETWEEN THE TWO PICS?

ANSWERS

WHICH PLAYER SCORED? "B".

MANAGER'S REMARK WELL DONE!

FAMOUS TEAMS

```
        L   WO
        I   D
    CELT   E   WIMBLED
V   R    O B
I   A    U L
L   N    M C
L   G    O
A   E   H
    R   T
C   S
I
T
ASTON VILLA
LEEDS
COVENTRY
```

FOUR-LETTER WORDS
— Aero, amen, atom, earn, mane, mate, mean, meat, moan, moat, more, mute, name, near, neat, rant, rate, ream, rent, roam, rota, rout, tame, team, tern, tart, tent, tear, tone, tour, tote, trot, true, torn, turn, tune, are 37.

WORD LADDER
— SHOT, SOOT, COOT, COAT, GOAT, GOAL.

DIFFERENCES
The five differences are — the striker's number; fan's banner; defender's sock; part of goal missing; and goalie's jersey.

TERRY'S TORNADOES

Thirteen-year-old Terry Miller's "Tornadoes" were playing in a preliminary round of the Barnston Boys Cup . . .

FIVE MINUTES LEFT . . . THREE-ALL!

83

Fifteen minutes from the end Terry made it two one, the final score!

GOOD ONE!

The Tornadoes were elated by their victory. But there was further excitement for Terry and Billy . . .

WOULD YOU AND TYSON BE AVAILABLE FOR A COUNTY SELECT? THE FINAL DECISION WOULD DEPEND ON HOW YOU PLAY IN THE FINAL.

GEE, WOULD I?

I'M SORRY, I WON'T MAKE IT.

'S A SHAME, BILLY. IT'S A GREAT HONOUR TO BE ASKED.

YEH, BUT MY AUNTS . . . I COULDN'T RISK IT.

The official made some enquiries and the following evening . . .

. . . MARVELLOUS LITTLE PLAYER. HE SURELY MUST BE AVAILABLE FOR THE COUNTY SELECT.

WHAT ARE YOU TALKING ABOUT? BILLY DOESN'T PLAY FOOTBALL.

OH-OH!

The whole story came out — and the result was, the indignant aunts banned Billy from even playing in the final. A council of war was held . . .

MY AUNTS WILL NEVER FORGIVE ME. DECEITFUL BOY THEY CALLED ME.

DON'T WORRY, WE'LL THINK OF SOMETHING . . .

SILLY OLE CUCKOOS! HOW CAN WE BEAT CANAL STREET RAIDERS WITHOUT YOU? THEY WON THEIR SEMI THREE NIL! THEY'VE THE BEST DEFENCE IN BARNSTON!

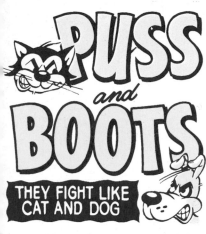

PUSS and BOOTS

THEY FIGHT LIKE CAT AND DOG

HMM... I WONDER IF I CAN BE ANY HELP... OR SOMETHING...

TODAY!!! THE GREAT BOOTS WILL DEMONSTRATE HIS SKILL— HE CAN ESCAPE FROM ANYTHING

LATER—

NOW, IF SOME KIND MEMBER OF THE AUDIENCE WILL HELP TIE ME UP, I SHALL ESCAPE IN TWO SECONDS FROM THIS LOCKED MAIL-BAG, CHAINED UP, IN THE TRUNK AND SUSPENDED FROM THE TREE!

PERMIT ME, O FURRY SAUSAGE!

WHAT? YOU? JUST WATCH IT THEN—

WHEN I'M IN THE BAG, THIS HERE EXCUSE FOR A MOGGIE WILL LOCK IT USIN' THE LOCKS I'VE GIVEN HIM! THINKS—'COS THEY'RE TRICK LOCKS!

CAN YOU HEAR ME, MUTT? I'M GONNA USE THESE EXTRA-STRONG NON-TRICK LOCKS THAT I'VE BROUGHT!

MUFFLED VOICE— EH? WHATZAT? HANG ON A MINUTE!

RIGHT! NOW LET'S SEE YOU GET OUT OF THAT LOT!

!

HOURS LATER—

RIGHT OVER LEFT, NO, NO, IT'S LEFT OVER RIGHT, OR IS IT...? I'LL BE OUT OF HERE IN TWO SECONDS IF IT TAKES ME ALL YEAR!

WE MAY AS WELL GO HOME, LADS... THIS LOOKS LIKE BEING A LONG JOB!

MORNING CAME AT LAST!

THAT MOGGIE! GRRR!

REVENGE

LATER— HEE-HEE! I'LL LET OLD FUZZY-FACE DOWN NOW AND PUNCH HIM ON THE NOSE—HE'LL BE TOO WEAK TO FIGHT BACK!

STRANGE... HE'S VERY QUIET... HE MUST BE HAVING A SNOOZE! COME OUT AND FIGHT LIKE A COWARD!

CREAK!

BOOM!

AND SOON—

HEY, TICH! ARE YOU TAKING AN OLD EGYPTIAN MUMMY TO THE MUSEUM? HO-HO-HO!

BAGGLE!

VERY FUNNY! IT'S JUST AS WELL MY DEAR NEPHEW'S BUSY OR I'D SET HIM ON YOU TO DUFF YOU UP!

B-B-BAGGLE?!!

93

Did you hear about the man who slept with his head under the pillow? When he woke up he discovered that the fairies had taken all his teeth!

"Fat Willie's doctor put him on a diet for three months. All he had to eat and drink were bananas and coconut milk."
"Did he lose any weight?"
"Nope! But he can't half climb trees!"

WEIGHT LIFTING MADE EASY by Everard Muscles.

HAIR CARE by Dan Druff.

THE HAUNTED HOUSE by Hugo First.

QUAINT ENGLISH FOLK CUSTOMS by Morris Dancer.

SPACE WARS by Ray Gunn.

QUICK SNACKS by Sandy Widge.

BATTY BOOKS

What's black and hairy and is surrounded by water?
A North Sea oil wig!

Doctor! Doctor! I've swallowed a roll of film! Just lie down in a darkened room and see if anything develops!

A man went to the dentist, sat in the chair and immediately began yelling his head off: "Calm down," said the dentist. "I haven't touched your tooth yet!" "I know," the man replied, "but you're standing on my foot!"

Is it difficult to bury a dead elephant?
Yes! It's a huge undertaking.

Local (to American Tourist): Aye! This is the Forth Bridge! Tourist: Gee! What happened to the other three?

What did the judge say when he came home in the evening? "It's been a very trying day!"

How do you stop a cold going to your chest? Tie a knot in your neck!

Teddy Bear went to work on a building site. He'd only been there an hour when he complained to the foreman that his pick had been stolen. "I'm not surprised," said the foreman. "Didn't you know that today's the day that teddy bears have their picks nicked?"

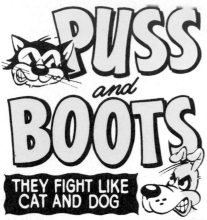

PUSS and BOOTS

THEY FIGHT LIKE CAT AND DOG

HEH-HEH! THAT MOGGIE IS GONNA GET THE SHOCK OF HIS MISERABLE, FLEA-INFESTED LIFE!

CYCLISTS THIS WAY

HALF A NIRDLE LATER—

GOOD-NESS! THERE MUST BE ROAD-WORKS AHEAD! I MUST TURN OFF!

INNOCENT SUCKER

CYCLISTS THIS WAY

IT'S WORKING!

WOO-HOO-HOO! I'M A GENIUS! A GENUINE £4 CARAT GOLD-ENCRUSTED GENIUS! NOT TO MENTION HAN'SOME!

TOOTIE TOOTSIE I HATE BOOTSIE!

DUCK!

FREE CYCLE PARK

COO! WHAT A STEEP HILL! AND SUCH A NARROW LITTLE ROAD! THE COUNCIL SHOULD DO SOMETHING ABOUT THIS!

PHEW!

PUFF!

GASP!

PECH!

R-R-RUMBLE! R-R-RUMBLE!

EH? WHASSAT? HUH? SHRIEK!

R-R-RUMBLE!

ER.... PEEP-PEEP!

AAARGH! MERCY! THEY'RE GAINING ON ME! SCREAM!

BOP!

CALL THE AIR-FORCE! CALL THE FIRE-BRIGADE! CALL A DOCTOR!

IT'S ALL RIGHT, HE HASN'T HURT HIMSELF. HE'S LANDED ON HIS HEAD!

GRAGH!

WHUMP!

WELL, I DON'T NEED A CRYSTAL BALL TO WORK OUT WHO DID THAT! WHERE'S HE GOING... AHA!

£5 CHALLENGE BY THE GORILLA!

AHA!

NOW, THEN! WHAT LUCKY LAD IS GOING TO WIN HIMSELF A NICE CRISP FIVER BY LASTING THREE MINUTES IN THE RING WITH THIS 'ERE DEAR LITTLE MAN-EATING OVER-GROWN CHIMP WOT HASN'T BEEN FED THIS WEEK?

COO! YOU WOULDN'T CATCH ME IN THERE! NOT LIKELY!

HUH?

DANGLE

A FIVER! OH, BOY! 'S MINE!

AHA! WE HAVE A VICTIM... ER... CHALLENGER!

EH? NO, NO, I DIDN'T... I MEAN...THAT FIVER... ER... HELP!

HUP!

SNARL!

GRRRR!

AARGH! HELP!

PUNCH!

BOP!

MERCY!

BASH! TWIST!

SCREAM!

OOH! ME TOE-BONE!

WELL, WELL, IF IT ISN'T MY OLD FRIEND, BOOTS, LOOKING AS HANDSOME AS EVER! HAVE AN ACCIDENT?

NO THANKS, I'VE JUST HAD ONE... GROAN...

DAINTY DROP

Morgyn the Mighty, the strongest man in the
world, was in the wilds of Borneo . . .

A MAN OF THE WOODS CAUGHT IN A BAG TRAP! AND THAT IS NO ORDINARY NET OF HEMP OR SISAL!

STEEL WIRE. THOSE WHO SET THIS KNOW THE STRENGTH OF AN ORANG-UTAN!

ROAM FREE, WILD COUSIN.

A SHOT!

MAY AS WELL TAKE THIS OTHER FINE SAMPLE OF FAUNA, BOGAN.

YES, HERR DOKTOR.

A HYPO-DART! SOME KIND OF DRUG!

THE CROCS HAVE HIM, HERR DOKTOR.

A DEPLORABLE WASTE OF A FINE SPECIMEN. HOWEVER, WE HAVE THE OTHER.

Morgyn had reached shelter . . .

A LAUNCH — AH, THOSE TWO MEN. THEY TRAVEL UPRIVER — AH, MY MIND CLOUDS OVER . . .

Morgyn lay unconscious for an hour — then a python spotted him . . .

He awoke — just in time!

A PYTHON — AND HUNGRY!

MY STRENGTH IS BACK — THE DRUG HAS WORN OFF!

Morgyn hurled the python from him and it slithered off . . .

I DO NOT LIKE SUCH MEN AS THOSE IN MY BACKYARD. I MUST LEARN ABOUT THEM.

Morgyn fashioned a raft . . .

A LAKE — AND DYAK LONGHUTS.

101

A faint sound made Morgyn turn . . .

DOCTOR RAVEL! THE REPORTS OF YOUR DEATH WOULD APPEAR EXAGGERATED.

THEY WERE ARRANGED BY MYSELF TO LEAVE ME FREE TO DO THE WORK THAT SO ANGERED LESSER MEN. THAT MOB ACTUALLY TRIED TO KILL ME SIMPLY FOR DOING VALUABLE EXPERIMENTS ON THE CRIMINALLY INSANE.

I UNDERSTAND YOUR WORK INVOLVED BIO-CYBERNETIC ENGINEERING — THE LINKING OF MAN AND MACHINE.

BOGAN, PUT AWAY YOUR PISTOL. THIS IS OBVIOUSLY A MOST UNUSUAL WILD MAN — ONE WITH THE LEARNING AND INTELLECT TO APPRECIATE THE MARCH OF SCIENCE.

YOU SHALL SEE IT ALL, MY NEW FRIEND. THAT CABIN IS THE TURBINE HOUSE OF THE OLD MINE. ITS OUTPUT IS SMALL, YET ADEQUATE FOR MY NEEDS.

THE MAN OF THE WOODS I TRIED TO SAVE.

THE RAW MATERIAL OF MY WORK HERE. I SHALL SHOW YOU WHAT SCIENCE MAY MAKE OF THIS OTHERWISE USELESS CREATURE.

MY LABORATORY — AND MY CREATIONS. TWO WILD CREATURES SUCCESSFULLY LINKED TO A COMPUTER WHICH AT THE MOMENT HAS THEM DE-ACTIVATED — OR SOUNDLY SLEEPING.

Understanding came to Morgyn — too late!

YES — YOU. A WILD MAN WHO SHALL BE THE FIRST OF THE NEW RACE OF MAN AND COMPUTER JOINED AS ONE — A CYBORG.

BOGAN, HOW FORTUNATE I AM READY WITH THE MORE REFINED IMPLANT SUITED TO A MAN.

HERR DOKTOR — LOOK!

THE WILD MAN BREAKS FREE!

SUCH IMPRESSIVE STRENGTH WILL BE USEFUL. HOWEVER, FIRST HE MUST BE SUBDUED.

AWAKEN, MY BEAUTIES.

NOW YOU WILL SEE HOW THEY PERFORM A SIMPLE TASK, WILD MAN.

I CANNOT HARM POOR CREATURES IN SUCH A CONDITION.

YOU HAVE NO ESCAPE, WILD MAN. THEY WILL RUN YOU DOWN AND BRING YOU BACK.

THE TURBINE HOUSE! WHAT WILL HAPPEN IF I CUT OFF THE ELECTRICITY?

HERE THEY COME. NO TIME TO MESS ABOUT TRYING SWITCHES!

Summoning up all his strength, Morgyn wrenched the generator from its mountings!

THEY HAVE HALTED. THEY JUST STAND AND STARE AT ME.

NOW THEY WALK AWAY . . .

. . . AND ENTER THE DARKENED MINE.

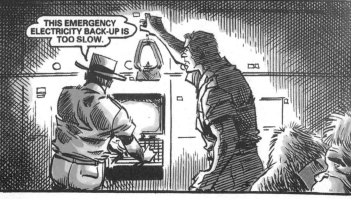

THIS EMERGENCY ELECTRICITY BACK-UP IS TOO SLOW.

HERR DOKTOR — THE BEASTS! LOOK AT THEIR EYES!

OUT OF CONTROL AND REVERTED TO NATURAL SAVAGERY. SHOOT, YOU FOOL — SHOOT THEM!

Bogan fired again and again, but still the orang-utans came on!

AYEEEEEEEEEEEEEEH!

THAT SOUNDS HUMAN — AND THE SHOOTING HAS STOPPED!

The lights suddenly came on . . .

ALL DEAD! THE MAD SCIENTIST AND HIS HANDIWORK DESTROYED.

Morgyn released the caged orang-utan . . .

AWAY YOU GO, MAN OF THE WOODS. I HAVE SOMETHING TO DO BEFORE I FOLLOW.

Later . . .

FIRE IS THE BEST WAY OF CLEANSING SUCH EVIL!

The End

TORO
SPACE SAMURAI

It is the future. Toro Tanaka and his crewman Rat roamed the galaxy fighting oppression — but now they were under attack!

THE OUTLAW TANAKA! ZAP HIM!

HE'S AS GOOD AS DEAD, CAPTAIN.

...oro did some investigating...

IT'S AN OLD SPACE FREIGHTER CRACKED OPEN BY A CRASH LANDING. THE WRECKAGE HAS BEEN LOOTED — BY SURVIVORS MAYBE.

UNLESS THIS PLANET DOES HAVE INHABITANTS, BOSS.

Next morning...

WIDENING MY SEARCH LOOP, RAT. ARE YOU SURE YOU WOULDN'T LIKE TO TAKE OVER FOR A BREAK?

A TEMPTING OFFER, BUT WORK COMES FIRST, BOSS. I GOT LOTS HERE TO KEEP ME BUSY.

...oro had taken out the shuttle...

COMING UP TO ANOTHER LAKE. WAIT — YES, I SEE MOVEMENT!

LIFE — AND IT'S NOT HUMAN. THE ODD THING IS THAT THE CREATURES DON'T APPEAR TO BE ALARMED BY THE SHUTTLE.

ME FRIEND. YOU UNDERSTAND.

THEY ACT FRIENDLY, BUT THEY DON'T SEEM TO SPEAK TERRAN.

THIS IS STRANGE, RAT. LIZARD INFANTS WHO UNDERSTAND HIGHER MATHEMATICS!

Then...

SOMETHING THAT SPEAKS TERRAN — A SHIPBOARD ROBO-MECH, RAT.

HURRY! BE QUICKER.

STOP WHIPPING THESE PEOPLE.

I OBEY ORDERS. KINDLY DO NOT INTERFERE.

YOU SHOULD LISTEN TO FRIENDLY ADVICE, MISTER!

MALFUNCTION! MALFUNCTION!

ONE BADLY RATTLED ROBO-MECH. I'LL FOLLOW HIM AND SEE WHERE HE GOES, RAT.

HE'S HEADING INTO A SMALL VALLEY. I SEE SOME CULTIVATED GROUND, LIZARDFOLK AT WORK AND NOW SOMETHING INTERESTING . . . .

A HOUSE AND A HUMAN BEING, RAT. I'M PUTTING DOWN.

AT LAST, A HUMAN FACE. I'M WIL CHUX, THE ONLY SURVIVOR WHEN THE FLEET SUPPLY SHIP "TRANSIT-NINE" DITCHED FOUR YEARS BACK — APART FROM TWO ROBO-MECHS. YOU CAN SEE I'VE SETTLED IN PRETTY WELL.

I NOTICE YOU APPEAR TO BE PROVIDING WORK FOR THE LOCAL NATIVES.

THE LIZARDS! OH YEAH, A DIM LOT, BUT USEFUL LABOUR. I'VE HAMMERED SOME ROUGH FARMING AND A FEW OTHER SKILLS INTO THEIR THICK SKULLS.

FIRMNESS IS ALL THAT'S NEEDED. YOU JUST HAVE TO SHOW THE REPTILES WHO IS BOSS.

SO I SEE.

110

In February, 1943, during the Second World War, the 77th Indian Infantry Brigade crossed over the Chindwin River into Burma. When they emerged from the jungle some ten to twelve weeks later, their fame had spread round the world — they were the Chindits! Named after the stone Burmese lions that guarded the temples, the Chindits had marched through the almost impenetrable jungle in seven separate columns with the aim of disrupting the Japanese lines of communication.

ACTION STATIONS!
A TRUE WAR STORY

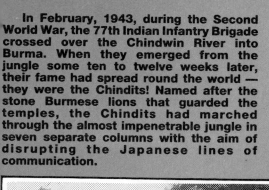

They headed for their main objective, the Mandalay-Myitkyina railway, 150 miles behind the Japanese lines, carrying heavy packs and with their remaining supplies on mules. Some of the columns were detected and had to fight their way through, but most made it and set about destroying the vital Jap supply route. Charges were set and the raiders withdrew to safety as the line was destroyed in 75 places over a stretch of 30 miles. The Chindits moved deeper behind the enemy lines but the Japs had assembled a huge force to track them down and eventually the raiders were forced to scatter and head back for India.

Most of the Chindits had marched 1000 miles through the jungle — but it had been worth it! A large Japanese army had been tied up hunting for them and a vital supply route had been disrupted.

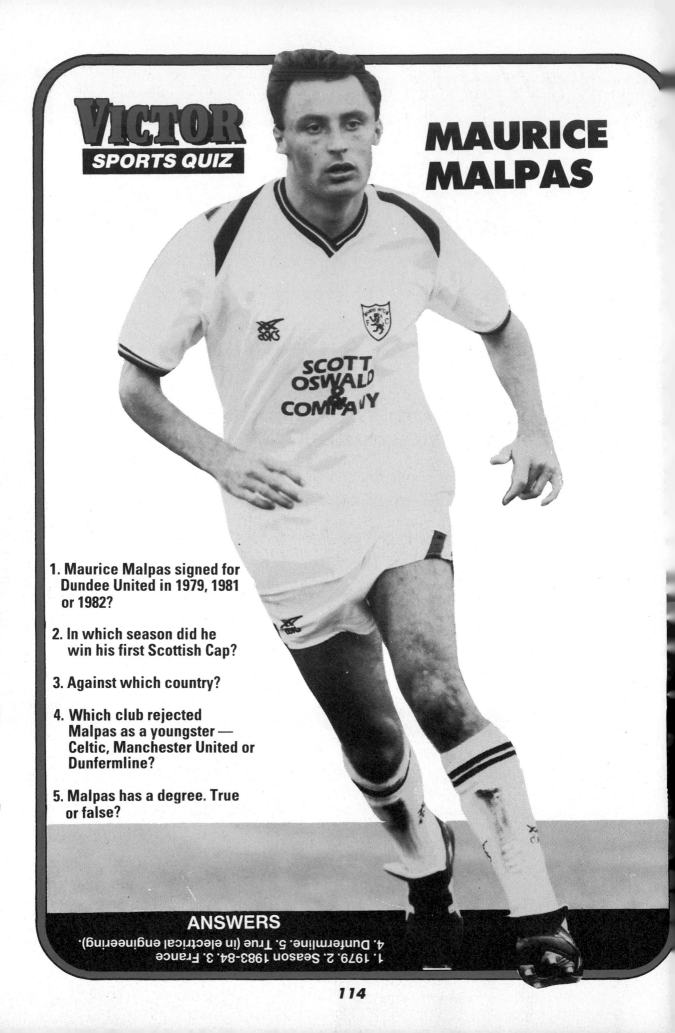

VICTOR SPORTS QUIZ

MAURICE MALPAS

1. Maurice Malpas signed for Dundee United in 1979, 1981 or 1982?

2. In which season did he win his first Scottish Cap?

3. Against which country?

4. Which club rejected Malpas as a youngster — Celtic, Manchester United or Dunfermline?

5. Malpas has a degree. True or false?

SOME OF THIS TURKISH GRUB'S BETTER'N OUR OWN RATIONS!

SCOFF IT UP, THEN, DELANEY! YOU'RE WANTED!

I'M FROM BRIGADE INTELLIGENCE. THOSE ENEMY DESPATCHES YOU CAPTURED MUST BE DELIVERED TO OUR MAJOR MAXON AT KARZAK.

WHERE MIGHT THAT BE, SIR?

IN THE HAMRA HILLS. I'LL SHOW YOU ON THE MAP. OUR OFFICER THERE ORGANISES KHARGUL TRIBESMEN TO MAKE RAIDING ATTACKS ON THE ENEMY.

NO GOOD NIGHT'S KIP FOR US, SNAPPER! MY BLINKING FAULT FOR CHASING THAT TURK!

WE'RE BEING FIRED ON! LIKELY SOME TURKS WHO BOLTED FROM THAT CAMP.

I'LL TAKE COVER IN THIS DRY WADI.

But later . . .

LET HIM PASS! HE'S ONLY A BUGLER! FIRE AT THE TROOPERS HE LEADS!

FOOLED 'EM INTO SHOOTING AT SHADOWS!

At dawn . . .

THIS IS STEEP! WISH YOU WERE A MOUNTAIN MULE, SNAPPER?

NOW ARE THOSE ROCKS JUST FALLING — OR BEING PUSHED?

PUSHED! BY UNFRIENDLY LOCALS!

HALT OR WE SHOOT!

THIS IS NO PLACE FOR ME TO FIGHT OR RUN, CHUMS! BUT AREN'T THOSE BRITISH RIFLES?

THE BRITISH GIVE US GUNS AND SUPPLIES. WE ARE KHARGULS.

THEN YOU MUST BE CHUMS OF MAJOR MAXON AT KARZAK?

Soon, at a hill village . . .

THE BRITISH OFFICER IS IN THERE.

CAPTURED ENEMY DESPATCHES, MAJOR MAXON.

NO USE BRINGING THEM TO ME!

A TURKISH OFFICER!

CAPTAIN RAHMAN. I AM HIS PRISONER HERE — AND SO ARE YOU NOW!

THESE ARE MERELY PAPERS ADVISING ALL OUR UNITS THAT THE KHARGUL TRIBESMEN ARE NOW OUR ALLIES.

MEANING THESE LOCALS HAVE SWOPPED SIDES!

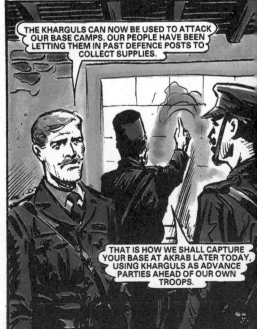

THE KHARGULS CAN NOW BE USED TO ATTACK OUR BASE CAMPS. OUR PEOPLE HAVE BEEN LETTING THEM IN PAST DEFENCE POSTS TO COLLECT SUPPLIES.

THAT IS HOW WE SHALL CAPTURE YOUR BASE AT AKRAB LATER TODAY, USING KHARGULS AS ADVANCE PARTIES AHEAD OF OUR OWN TROOPS.

Delaney was escorted out under guard . . .

I'VE LANDED IN A RIGHT PICKLE HERE!

GOOD HORSE, TOMMY!

TOO GOOD TO LET THOSE RASCALS RIDE HIM!

HERE, SNAPPER!

AAAH!

LOOK OUT!

HUP! GET GOING!

MAY AS WELL TRY A RUN FOR IT!

122

A BATTERY OF OUR THIRTEEN-POUNDER FIELD GUNS.

INDIAN ARMY LADS. TOUGH SCRAPPERS!

JUST A PRACTICE SHOOT ON DEFENCE LINES. WE CEASED FIRE WHEN WE SPOTTED YOU COMING. ANY MESSAGE FOR US?

I'D BEST DELIVER IT TO THE COMMANDER AT AKRAB, SIR.

A BIG SUPPLY DUMP! WHERE'S YOUR C.O., SARGE?

OVER THERE. COLONEL HARDY.

KHARGULS FIGHTING FOR THE TURKS NOW? NONSENSE! DID MAJOR MAXON SEND YOU WITH A WRITTEN DESPATCH?

HOW COULD HE, SIR, WHEN HE'S A PRISONER OF THE TURKS?

OUR SCOUTS HAVE REPORTED KHARGUL TRIBESMEN MOVING DOWN THE SHATTRA VALLEY. THEY COME HERE FOR SUPPLIES. I CERTAINLY DO NOT INTEND TO TREAT THEM AS ENEMIES ON YOUR SAY SO. DISMISSED, DELANEY!

BLINKING STAFF OFFICERS! WON'T BELIEVE ANYTHING UNLESS IT'S ON OFFICIAL DESPATCH PAPER! AND THEY OBVIOUSLY DIDN'T GET ANY MESSAGE FROM THAT BRIGADE INTELLIGENCE BLOKE! THIS LOT'LL BE CAUGHT NAPPING GOOD 'N' PROPER!

Out on the valley hillside . . .

HERE COME THE KHARGULS TO FOOL OUR DEFENCES — THE TURKISH TROOPS WON'T BE FAR BEHIND 'EM!

A FIELD TELEPHONE WIRE TO THAT INDIAN GUN BATTERY — THAT GIVES ME AN IDEA!

Back at the gun position . . .

ORDERS FROM AKRAB HQ, SIR. OPEN FIRE TO STOP THOSE TRIBESMEN. TOO URGENT FOR WRITTEN ORDERS.

WHY SEND YOU WHEN WE ARE IN TOUCH BY FIELD TELEPHONE?

LINE'S DEAD, SIR, PROBABLY CUT.

THAT EXPLAINS THE DESPATCH RIDER! OPEN DEFENSIVE FIRE!

BRITISH GUNS! FIRING TO STOP US!

A Turkish commander also watched . . .

THE BRITISH MUST KNOW OUR PLANS. ORDER FULL ATTACK!

THEY'RE CHARGING US! NOT SO FRIENDLY NOW, ARE THEY, SIR?

IF THIS DOESN'T WAKE 'EM UP AT AKRAB HQ, NOTHING WILL!

At the supply camp . . .

SO THAT DESPATCH RIDER WAS RIGHT, COLONEL?

YES, BY GAD! TURKISH TROOPS MOVING UP BEHIND THE KHARGULS! ALERT ALL DEFENCE POSTS!

AAAGH!

HOPELESS! CALL OFF THE ASSAULT!

Later . . .

WE ARE IN SIGNAL CONTACT WITH AKRAB HQ AGAIN. COLONEL HARDY CONGRATULATES US ON OUR ACTION HERE. WILL YOU BE REPORTING BACK TO HIM?

NO KNOWING IF THOSE STAFF OFFICERS WOULD GIVE US A MEDAL OR A COURTMARTIAL, SNAPPER!

NO, I'LL BE RETURNING TO MY OWN UNIT NOW, SIR.

125

THE END

FACT FII

HEIGHT: 4 ft. 11 in.
HOBBIES: Anything to with football.
FAVE FOOD: Same as Jimmy Grant's.
AMBITION: To score g like Jimmy!
PET HATE: Losing games.

TERRY "TORNADOE MILLI

FACT FILE

HEIGHT: 5 ft. 8 in.
HOBBIES: Tinkering with bikes.
FAVE FOOD: Any FAST food!
AMBITION: To stay at the top in motor-cycling.
PET HATE: My bike breaking down yards from the winning flag!

GARY "BIKER" JONES